"The real substance of '37 Th [illegible] There is a spirit of truth through [illegible] ..cription of each thing. His enthusiasm for pursuing life and business is infectious...this brother knows what he's talking about."

—Los Angeles Sentinel

"Anyone who even suspects that changing their thinking can revolutionize their life should read this book... perhaps twice. It may change many of your important relationships, especially the one with prosperity."

—Nelson Davis
Nelson Davis Television Productions

"The book moves you to think positively and to take a look at yourself from a winning view, even if you feel you have nothing going on."

—Harold Lee Rush
Host/WJPC

"A lighthearted yet thoughtful trek through some very important ideas. 37 Things ... hits one nail on the head after another. "

—Issues & Views

"I am very impressed! Wonderful work! Well done!"

—Dr. Robert Schuller
Crystal Cathedral

"...this is a worthwhile work. Do buy this book, read it, and pass it on....."
—Houston Sun

"There are new, fresh voices in the black community. Errol Smith is one of the most intelligent and challenging of these voices."
—David Horowitz
Activist, Best Selling Author

"Written in a straightforward shoot from the hip style which puts into words thoughts that many black men have but refuse to verbalize for fear of being wrongfully labeled a 'sell out'. The book provides a blueprint which black men can use to break free of the stereotypes which bind us."
—Daniel Colimon
President/Law-In-Motion, Inc.

"When I read this book, I was astounded by the insight. Quite frankly, these are equally as beneficial to people of other races because his insights really go to the core of success in anybody's life."
—Mills Crenshaw
Talk Show Host/KKTK

37 THINGS EVERY BLACK MAN NEEDS TO KNOW

© Copyright 1991 by Errol Smith

Library of Congress Catalog Card Number: 91-176884

ISBN: 0-9625578-1-1

E185.86.S65

All rights reserved. No portion of this book may be reproduced, mechanically, electronically, or by any other means, including photocopying-without the written permission of the publisher.

St. Clair René Publishing
24307 Magic Mountain Parkway, Suite 285
Valencia, CA 91355

Fifth Printing

Cover design by Jeannette Smith
Photo by Darius Anthony

Other Products by Errol Smith

All The Right Questions
How to Ask For What You Want & Get It

The Antidote to Racism

Living Well is the Best Revenge

Order Form in Back

If you would like Errol to speak at your business, school or oganization or to receive a multiple order discount for "37 Things Every Black Man Needs to Know," please call: (818) 507-6484.

TABLE OF CONTENTS

PART I - HOW TO DEAL WITH THE PROBLEMS OF BEING BLACK IN WHITE AMERICA

PART II - MONEY AND BUSINESS

PART III - WHAT HOLDS BLACK MEN DOWN AND WHAT TO DO ABOUT IT

IV - A FEW MORE THINGS
- QUICKIES -

V - ONE LAST THING

INTRODUCTION

For years you've been told how important it is to know that Abraham Lincoln freed the slaves, that George Washington is the father of our country, and that Christopher Columbus discovered America (of course, the Indians were already here but apparently they didn't count). By now, you're pretty sure that 2 + 2 = 4, and that what goes up must come down. But somewhere between kindergarten and mid-life crisis, you ask yourself the ultimate question, "*So what? * Why do I need to know all of this anyway?"

It seems like all of our lives people have been trying to teach us things we felt we really didn't need to know; while the things we *really* wanted to know no one was teaching. Things like: what do other guys say to women when they slow dance? What's the best way to eat ribs in public? What should you do with your eyes in a crowded elevator? And how do you stop those little in-grown hair bumps from popping up all over your face?

By now, most of us have found the answers to these questions. But there are some other things important to black men for which we still don't have the answers.

It is well documented that there is a crisis within the black community. Vast numbers of black men are being lost to drugs, homicide, or a life of crime that lands them in prison.

Sociologists, psychologists, theologians, and politicians vary on their beliefs as to the causes and the solutions to these problems.

Born in Harlem and raised in inner city New York, I started on the other side of the tracks, but I moved *through* the urban black experience into Mainstream America—where I've managed to do very well in business.

In the process, I've received some incredible lessons about what it really takes for a black man to survive and succeed in America. I found that there were beliefs I held that had to be changed, new concepts that had to be learned, and a number of new skills that had to be developed.

But many of these new beliefs, concepts, and skills are not things you can learn in school. They are things that come *only through experience* or from someone who has experience.

Other cultures have traditionally used "mentors" to pass on to the "up & coming" the ideas, concepts, and skills they need to succeed. But in fatherless black homes, or homes where no black man in the family has made it, there is little that can be *passed down* or *passed on*.

As I look back along the road I've traveled, I see that the path was narrow and winding, difficult to get on, and difficult to follow. To navigate it successfully there are at least 37 *things that every black man needs to know.*

Things like how to deal with the burden and stigma of being born into a culture that most of the world sees as poor, uneducated and powerless.

Things like how to handle the inevitable conflict that comes from being black in America.

Things like what it is that *really* holds black men down and what to do about it.

This is not a book filled with intellectual mumbo-jumbo about the politics of being black in White America. It's not a book of theories from sociologists, psychologists, or political scientists. It's a book of practical information from a street smart business executive who has played the street games, the corporate games, and the entrepreneurial game—and won!

37 Things Every Black Man Needs to Know is meant to be a guide to every young black man in America. It's meant to be a handbook to give you the perspective and skills you'll need to make it. It's designed to be a book that's simple and straight forward, something you can carry around in your pocket or briefcase and refer to often. It's meant to be the "MENTOR" many black men never have!

This book will give you answers *though some of them you might not like.* This book will give you something to *think* about, something to *laugh* about, and something to *use* every day for the rest of your life.

This book is *fresh*! It's not the same old stuff you've already heard. I've taken a different approach, and though I don't expect you to swallow everything I've written here, I do hope you will at least taste it.

Bon appétit!

PART I

HOW TO DEAL WITH THE PROBLEMS OF BEING BLACK IN WHITE AMERICA

1

THE FIRST THING YOU NEED TO KNOW

I remember the picture clearly. A man in a green shirt, lying on the ground, dying of a stab wound to his chest. I watched from our apartment window, as the crowd gathered and police and medical technicians arrived. The word on the street was that the dying man had accidentally stepped on another man's brand new alligator shoes, so the man pulled out a knife and stabbed him.

"Say what? A man got killed over a pair of shoes!" Help me out—maybe I'm missing something here. Is this the kind of mistake that should cost a man his life?

To anyone with two eyes and a heartbeat, it's pretty obvious there's a lot of anger concentrated in the black community. You've seen it, haven't you? On one end, it's a simmering, burning resentment that shows itself in what some call, the *black attitude*." At the other end, it's a full blown, explosive black rage.

Some say this resentment and anger comes

from the frustration of trying to deal with the hand black people have been dealt in life, the burden of racism and prejudice, and the result of the social pressure that comes with being black. Others say that blacks are simply hostile and aggressive by nature.

Now I admit that I am not a sociologist, a psychologist, or a historian, so I don't know much about the source or cause of all this anger. What I *do* know is that there are a lot of black men out there who are mad as hell and don't know what to do about it.

> *Don't push me cause I'm close to the edge. I'm trying not to lose my head........ It's like a jungle sometimes; it makes me wonder how I keep from going under.*

The tune is called "The Message", a rap song that sums up the frustration and anger felt by many black men, frustration and anger which I clearly understand.

Yes, I know what it means to live with the stigma of being born into a culture that most of the world sees as poor, uneducated, and powerless. I know how it feels to deal with the pressure of being a black man in White America. It's very real to me how poverty, racism, and prejudice can make you mad, because I've felt the anger and have struggled to deal with it myself. Yes, I definitely understand the anger, but ultimately, I found that getting mad was a waste, an incredible, unfortunate waste.

Remember the sixties? Of course you do. Who could forget them? That was the decade we burned down our *own* neighborhoods. Now I always thought that destroying our communities was a lot like gouging out one eye to get back at the other, but in the seventies and eighties, we outdid ourselves: we progressed from destroying buildings to destroying each other. Today, *more of us* kill more and more of us every year (which by the way does a remarkable job of relieving the overcrowding in our cities though it does leave a few subtle side effects.)

If you look around, you'll see that "anger" is destroying the lives of many black men, black families, and black communities, which makes it very clear to me that *learning how to deal with this anger* is the very first thing a black man needs to know to succeed in America.

Now it took several years for me to discover the best way to deal with *my own* anger. In fact, I was 26 before I saw a poster hanging in a car wash that would provide the best answer I've found so far. Maybe you've seen it—it's a picture of a man in front of the Department of Welfare, sitting proudly on a classic Bentley, smugly sipping champagne.

The poster is titled "Poverty Sucks", and when I saw the print, it instantly sparked something inside of me.

Somehow that picture and caption said it all. It expressed the anger I felt about being one of the "have nots", while at the same time expressed my desire to have it all. There was something in the smug look on that man's face which helped me to imagine how sweet it would be to rise above my conditions. Every time I saw it, my frustration and anger were turned into desire and drive. Then, one day, the answer came:

—Don't Get Mad, Get Motivated—

Bingo! Suddenly I realized that after years of getting mad, black men still weren't getting very far. I saw clearly that getting mad was a waste and that if we were ever going to get ahead, we'd have to *stop* getting mad and *start* getting busy--so I got busy!

I bought that print and hung it where I could see it often. Every time I felt frustrated, discouraged, or angry I looked at it, and year after year it inspired me. It helped me to convert my anger to motivation—motivation I used to stay busy reading, studying, and searching for ways to improve my life—ways I eventually found.

Several years later my friends and I created our own version of that print. In our print, I'm sitting on a brand new Rolls Royce Corniche in front of a beautiful mansion. The caption says, "Living Well is the Best Revenge." We later mass produced these prints and sold them all across the country.

One day, after a motivational rally, I was approached by Jeff, a very enthusiastic, young man who had previously purchased one of our prints. Jeff thanked me for producing the prints and told me he found it very motivational. He summed up his feelings this way:

> *"Anytime I feel discouraged or upset, I stare at my print till I feel better. It always reminds me of where I'm going, what I have to do to get there, and how great I'm gonna feel when I make it."*

I was so excited as I listened to his story that I could hardly contain myself. The poster was doing exactly what I had hoped it would— it was helping at least one other black man to practice the valuable secret I had been so fortunate to discover. The secret that *every black man* needs to know to succeed in America:

*"Don't Get Mad, Get Motivated—
Then Get Busy!"*

2
MOVE ON

Flip Wilson used to do a comedy routine about a church he called, "THE CHURCH OF THE WHAT'S HAPPENING NOW". He'd start every service by saying, "At this church, you won't hear much about what happened yesterday, because at this church we're here to talk about what's happening *now*." I like that word "now". I believe it's a very important word for black men.

But as one man told me, "It's hard *not* to get mad when you look back at what black men have been through in this country." I said, "Fine, then don't look back." You see, too many of us are stuck in the past; we're hung up on what happened yesterday.

Sure it's terrible that black men were forcibly taken from their land and sold into bondage. And, of course, it's sad that so much black culture and tradition were lost, and no it wasn't right that you were discriminated against when you applied for that job or tried to lease that apartment..., but all that happened yesterday.

I frequently meet black men who are dragging

the past around with them. Their conversation inevitably returns to what the white man has done to us and to how we've been held back. Some of them are so obssessed with what happened to blacks in the past that they spend their *present* studying and researching it. They talk about what black people *used* to be and how they *used* to live. Some even talk about going back to Africa.

Now this might be a culturally reckless thing for me to say, but I'm not interested in going back to Africa. Why should I be? I don't know many Italian Americans jumping on boats rushing back to Italy nor have I heard of a mass exodus of Irish scurrying back to Ireland. (Besides, what the heck would I look like standing on a corner in Johannesburg in a Lakers cap and an "I love L.A." sweat shirt).

When I do go to Africa, I'll go as a tourist or as a businessman and then I'll come **back to America**.

You see, I've found that you can't *move forward looking back*. To progress, you have to move on. The Japanese understood this. They didn't get stuck in what happened at Nagasaki and Hiroshima. They could have licked their wounds for at least a hundred years. Instead, they moved on and in less than 50 years, rebuilt their nation and became the leading economic power in the world. Sure there are differences between the Japanese experience and ours, but the principle still applies.

The Japanese demonstrated how quickly a people can turn their conditions around if they put their attention on moving on. This is why I'm *not* interested in spending a lot of time studying the past. I'm more interested in *living* my *present* and my *future*.

There are many black Americans who don't know a cotton picking thing about their past but are living a good *today* and building a better *tomorrow*. They have put their attention on what's happening **now** and what needs to be done **today**!

So how important are the injustices of yesterday? Not very. What should you know about slavery? Not much. How much do you really need to know about your roots? I say, not a lot. What you *do* need to know is how to move ahead in America, and the second step to moving ahead is *moving on!*

3

MOVE YOUR SHOULDERS
UP AND DOWN

I heard a great story the other day about Lionel Richie. According to the story, Lionel entered an elevator one day with his dog, Lady, and found a white woman already inside. As the door closed Lionel turned to his dog and commanded, "Lady, sit down!" Much to his surprise and embarrassment he saw his dog and the woman immediately drop to the floor. True story? I don't know, but it comically represents a reality that is all too familiar to most black men.

As a black man, there are certain things that come with the package. There will always be those who will clutch their bags, lock their doors, and pull down their blinds when they see you coming. There will be social situations where no one will speak to you unless you speak first and, occasionally, there will be those who won't respond even then.

There will be the "watermelon" jokes and the occasional "nigger" joke, and from time to time, they'll double check your identification before accepting your credit card or cashing your check.

One day, as you're standing outside a restaurant, you may even run into the patron, who will assume you're the valet and hand you the keys to park his car. (By the way, it doesn't make a difference who you are; I read that this happened once to Jesse Jackson).

I remember a discussion I had a few months ago with LaVell, a very good friend of mine, who was enraged by the fact that as he entered an elevator, an old lady clutched her bag. "What does she think I am," he said. "I'm standing there impeccably dressed in a $500.00 suit, and this lady thinks I'm a purse snatcher." Sound familiar?

I assured him it wouldn't be the last time something like that would happen, and I shared with him a lesson I had learned from my father.

"You see, there are many things in life that you can do nothing to change—there will always be people who will prejudge you. If you allow them to upset you, then you become the victim."

Yes, the potential for you to feel victimized is out there, but the good news is that you can be the victor—all you have to do is develop the ability to shrug. That's right—just move your shoulders up and down. Your ability to shrug is the most powerful skill you can develop to handle these kinds of situations. By shrug I mean the ability to ignore and desensitize yourself to these events. The most freeing realization you can have is the awareness that what *they* think of you really doesn't matter. It's what *you* think of *you* that counts. (Unless, of course, you believe that their opinion is more important than your own.)

Recently, I was on my way out of an elevator. I too was impeccably dressed. As the door opened, I saw several faces—all 15 shades lighter than my own. Cordially, I said, "Good morning," but not one person responded.   Frankly, I was stunned that no one returned my greeting but I quickly got over it.   I immediately shrugged and said to myself, "Who cares?" and walked away with a smile.

I flashed back to the incident later and thought about how this experience might have affected me in the past.   I was glad that I had finally learned to apply a very important principle in life —a principle called Mind Over Matter—

If You Don't Mind —It Doesn't Matter

4
WHAT'S IN A NAME

Steve Allen once said at a Redd Foxx Roast, "We'll march forward toward a better tomorrow as soon as separate groups like the blacks, the negroes, and the coloreds can get together to work out their differences." Real cute, Steve! But cuter still is the fact that it's true.

Remember the push among our people to be called black instead of colored or negro? I remember the NAACP being challenged to change its name, and I know there are at least a few of you who remember (and will admit to) being called nigger affectionately by someone close to you. Then, of course, there are Afro-Americans; African Americans, and Black Americans—all of which leaves us with this profound and significant question: What *should* our people be called? Brace yourself for the answer — *who cares*? Now if you just sat up in your seat and said "Wait a minute, I do," I have one more question for you—why? What difference does it really make?

I say it's not the label they put on the package, but what's in the box that counts. The truth is, I am not what you call me nor do I become something different because you change my name. Our sense of self should run much deeper than that. We all were taught this as children. Remember?

> *Sticks and stones may break my bones but words can never hurt me* (as long as you don't talk about my mama).

I believe we're much too sensitive on this subject. The first time a black man was called nigger, he should have laughed and said, "I love that name." It would probably have been the last time he ever heard it.

You see, handling the labels that people give you is another one of those issues of mind over matter; yes, only when you mind does it matter.

You can call me Ray, or you can call me Jay, or you can call me anything you want, as long as I'm happy, healthy, wealthy, and fulfilled. We have too much to do to get hung up on a name.

So let's take a tip from Shakespeare who said: "A rose by any other name would still smell just as sweet."

5

LEARN TO PLAY
THE HAND YOU GET

Okay, let's face it—most of us weren't born with
a silver spoon in our mouths. We came from the
other side of the tracks, and we don't have the
complexion that makes the connections in this
country. That's right—we're black men, born
into a world that isn't exactly fond of black men,
so what are we going to do about it?

A. Complain to anyone who will listen?

B. Push and protest for more affirmative action?

C. Withdraw from the white community
    and create a world where the black man
    is supreme?

D. Learn to play the hand you get?

Now, I'm sure it would have been nice to be born
into a culture where the men don't face the same
challenges that we do, and I imagine it's a lot
easier for those who don't have to be "above
average" just to be considered equal. But I
occasionally wonder, if many of us would have
developed the skills and strength of character

that has come through dealing with the challenges of being black.

You see, when you've been dealt a good hand, it takes very little skill to play it, but it takes considerable skill and talent to play a poor hand well.

As black men, it's critical that we learn to play the hand we get. This requires the ability to see possibilities where others see only problems. To see stepping stones where most see stumbling blocks. It's the ability to turn disadvantages into advantages.

Early in my sales career, I would go out on sales calls and find some prospects visibly shaken to see that they were getting ready to meet with a "black man." The initial moments of those meetings were often very uncomfortable. I routinely felt that I was at a tremendous disadvantage with these prospects, especially when I was competing against white sales representatives. Then I remembered that the first step in selling anything to anyone is to get their attention.

I had often listened to other sales people complain about being treated like "just another salesperson." They found it hard to develop the customer's interest because they never captured their prospect's attention. Suddenly, I realized that what I thought was a disadvantage was actually an advantage in disguise.

From that point on, every time I saw one of those surprised faces looking back at me, I reminded myself that I had just successfully captured their attention—now all I had to do was to create interest, desire, and action.

What a competitive edge!

When you're black in White America, it's easy to stand out. *To me,* that's an incredible advantage—*use it!*

This is the kind of thinking that led someone to look at lemons and see lemonade, to take dried out grapes and repackage them as raisins , to see in dehydrated plums something called a prune.

It certainly takes a little more effort, but if you learn to play the hand you get, you'll find your hand is good enough to play the game and win.

6

GET WHAT YOU WANT AND MAKE THEM HAPPY THEY GAVE IT TO YOU

When I was growing up, I didn't learn much about conflict resolution in school. In fact, I received only two lessons:

Lesson I: If someone doesn't agree with you, hit him.

Lesson II: If you don't agree with someone, duck.

It's clear that force can quickly resolve conflict, but early on, I discovered that force is just not right for everybody.

As a teen in high school, I was 4'11", 137 lbs. Every friend, relative, enemy and associate I had was bigger than I was. Seeing the casualties, from our daily school yard brawls, made it clear that I would have to find some other means of conflict resolution if I was ever going to ever see a cap and gown. Fortunately, I discovered the art of persuasion—what an incredible skill!

I began to study persuasion as a means of survival, but soon I began to see it as a way to get people much bigger, stronger, and more powerful than I was, to do what I wanted.

Now here's something every black man can use. In fact, I'm convinced that each of us should take a lesson or two in the fine art of persuasion. Why? Because the world we live in is filled with conflict and as a black man in America, you can be sure you'll get your share.

Your minority status in this country virtually assures that in most conflicts, you'll be out manned and out gunned—they'll be bigger, stronger and more powerful.

Of course, many of us are used to fighting against the odds. Most of us have been fighting against something all our lives. There are those who even enjoy a good knock down, drag out brawl—especially when they win the battle.

But let's say we fight for Fair Housing and get it but create animosity in the process, or win the conflict over equal employment but end up with resentment as a result; or perhaps by force, we get White America to "*do the right thing*," but must then rely on force to keep them doing it. Then, no matter how sweet the victory, we're losing the war.

Force is the ability to get what you want from people whether they like it or not. Persuasion is the art of getting people to give you what you want and be happy they did.

Americans don't like to be forced to do anything, so force is sure to create enemies. But persuasion creates allies, and in case you haven't noticed, when you're black in America, *you need all the allies you can get!*

7
TAKE A TIP FROM NABISCO

Oreo—that's what we call those who appear black on the outside but behave in ways we normally assign to whites.

This means a black man who chooses English over slang, classical music over rap, golf over basketball, Izod's over Dashikis, or a night at the theater over a night at the dance club.

To many black men, this choice simply means striving to broaden their horizons, improve the quality of their lives, and move from one socio-economic level to another. But the social pressures they feel as they strive to be upwardly mobile can be traumatic.

If you've decided to succeed in mainstream America, you're virtually assured to reach a point where you find yourself sandwiched. On one side are the whites who won't accept you because you've have not yet "arrived", and on the other side are the blacks who won't accept you because you're too far gone. You may find yourself feeling isolated—unable to fit in or belong. Under the pressure, you may even conclude that it's wrong (you know, "uppity") to try to move up, so to cope, you may decide to just accept your place in life.... **Don't!**

You see the truth is, moving from one socio-economic level to another, though possible, has always been difficult. It can be tough, no matter what color you are. (Remember the Beverly Hill-billies). You've heard for years that it's lonely at the top. Well, as you start your climb, you'll find it's pretty lonely *on the way to* the top as well.

There are many challenges that anyone climbing the social ladder must face. When you're black and upwardly mobile, the "oreo syndrome" is just another hurdle you'll have to get over, but you can get over this hurdle quickly if you take a tip from Nabisco.

You see they made it a point to never sell oreos by the cookie—they always come in packs. Like you, there are other men out there who happen to be black and have found themselves in the same squeeze. They, too, feel isolated and stuck in the middle. Many are looking for men on their level with whom they can identify.

So if you need some good company, you don't have to rely on the crabs in the barrel. There are other so called "oreos" out there. Go find yourself a pack, grab a glass of milk, and squeeze in!

8

SOME WILL, SOME WON'T SO WHAT?

Early one Sunday morning, I had an experience with my father that has stuck with me since it happened. We were on our way to a fishing trip when we stopped at a tiny restaurant in a small town to pick up some breakfast.

As we walked in, I looked at the waitress, then followed my father to the back of the restaurant where we found a table and took a seat.

We waited for the waitress to come and take our order for what I thought was an "extraordinary" amount of time. As we continued to wait, I grew more and more anxious, till finally I began to make a fuss. I was upset that we weren't being waited on and upset that my father wasn't demanding better service.

Then suddenly, the waitress appeared. She was dripping apologies from her lips and doing everything she could to make us feel at home. It turned out she had not seen us come in and sit down. She was very embarrassed and so was I. What I thought was a clear-cut case of discrimination turned out to be not so clear-cut.

I know sometimes it's hard to imagine how your experiences could possibly be anything but discrimination, but the truth is that often when we receive "extraordinary" treatment, it has nothing to do with discrimination at all. However, the first thing many of us think is: *"I'm being treated this way because I'm black."*

Well there are two important things I've discovered about white people which every black man needs to know:

1. Some will discriminate against you.
2. Some won't.

That's right; contrary to what some of us believe, all whites are not sitting at home drumming up ways to shut out the black man. Simply said, all whites are not racist. (I know that there is at least one person reading this book for whom this is a new revelation.)

Your challenge, as you go through life, is to avoid assuming discrimination and remain open minded enough to see each situation you encounter for what it really is.

I realize sometimes this is very difficult. You find yourself getting "extraordinary" treatment and you think: "If this is not discrimination, then what else could it be." Well, here's a list of possibilities you can draw from when you suspect discrimination and you're struggling to maintain your objectivity. Start with "This is not discrimination," then add to it:

1. She's probably suffering from P.M.S.
2. He just lost a family member.
3. She's having a bad week.
4. He lost big money on Wall St. today.
5. Her boss just reprimanded her.
6. He just received a speeding ticket.
7. Her car broke down and she had to take a bus to work.
8. His mother-in-law is spending the month.
9. His wife just ran off with the milk man....again!

and oh yes!

THE WAITRESS DIDN'T
SEE YOU COME IN.

9

EVIDENTLY THEY DON'T KNOW WHO YOU ARE

The Lakers were behind, but Earvin Johnson was now back in the game, and the crowd was anticipating a display of "magic".

There were three very Anglo men sitting behind us who had gone out of their way to maintain a slightly more than social distance from us all evening. Their non-verbal message was clear. "I don't know you; I don't want to know you; let's make believe we're not watching this game together."

But as Magic came into the game, two of the men became very excited. "All right!" one said, "Now we're going to see how this game is supposed to be played." The other started telling the third man about Magic's performance over the years, reciting a litany of his performance statistics I would not have expected from Chick Hearn. It was clear that these gentlemen "loved some" Magic Johnson. As I compared the obvious affinity they had for Magic Johnson with the lack of affinity they had for us, it reminded me of an interesting phenomenon I had discovered.

You see, over the years, I've found that many of the people I've met who were apparently racist discriminated against black people, not black individuals. This became more clear as I became close with people who said they didn't "feel comfortable" with blacks but had close black friends.

This puzzled me and caused me to look a little deeper. What I found was that many whites don't dislike blacks—they dislike blacks they don't know.

Understanding this little phenomenon can be very helpful when you're trying to deal with apparent racism. You see, most of us take racism personally—we feel unaccepted and personally rejected.

During my sales seminars, I teach those who attend how to deal with rejection. They're encouraged not to take rejection personally but to take it professionally. I say to them:

> "When you are rejected, it's impossible for them to be rejecting you, because they don't know who you are (and if they did they'd probably love you)."

So they're taught to smile when rejected and to say to themselves, *"Evidently they don't know who I am."* This technique is very freeing, and it works equally as well in life as it does in sales.

You see, there will always be 20% of the people out there who will reject you no matter what you do. Similarly, there is another 20% who will accept you in spite of yourself. It's the remaining 60% that we're really trying to deal with here.

When you accept that those 60%, who discriminate against you, "really don't know who you are," you'll be able to avoid taking it personally. But more importantly, you'll have the power to move beyond the generalities of racism and get in touch with the real people behind those white faces. There you'll be surprised to find that many of those who apparently don't like black people will love you!

10
ADJUST YOUR THINKING

There are a lot of black men walking around believing that America owes them something for the way it treated black men in the past. They believe that programs should be put in place to compensate and make amends for the many ways blacks have been short-changed. They live their lives looking for somebody to give back to them what they feel was taken. If you're one of those black men, then please hear this:

THE WORLD DOESN'T OWE YOU ANYTHING!

I've never met a truly successful black man who believed that it did, so *adjust your thinking*.

11

GOD BLESS THE CHILD
WHO HAS HIS OWN

I don't see discrimination as a racial issue. I see it as an issue of the *"have nots"*, relying on those who have to supply their needs. This reliance on others has produced what I call, The New Slavery—slavery by default.

This kind of slavery forces you to live in a neighborhood you don't like because it's the only place you can afford to live.

It's the kind of slavery that has you driving for an hour to a job you can't stand from a neighborhood you don't like, but it's the only place you can afford to live.

It causes you to work with people you don't enjoy, at a job you can't stand, that you drive an hour to get to, from a neighborhood you don't like, but it's the only place you can afford to live.

But the epitome of this New Slavery is that it pays you less than you're worth, to work with people you don't enjoy, at a job you can't stand, that you drive and hour to get to, from a neighborhood you don't like, but it's the only place you can afford to live.

To be free of discrimination you have to decide what you want and *get it yourself.* We call this self reliance and it's the only way to freedom.

If you rely on yourself, you can take your own affirmative action. You no longer have to depend on fair housing laws; you can live virtually anywhere you want.

If you rely on yourself, you won't have to worry about the quality of education. You can send your children to the best schools in the country.

If you rely on yourself, you won't have to worry about inferior health care as you'll be able to get the best medical treatment available.

When you decide what you want and rely on yourself to get it, you quickly discover two things: the first is that you *can* get what you want and the second is that God does bless the child who has his own.

How do we become more self reliant? Keep reading.

PART II

MONEY
AND
BUSINESS

12

PAY YOURSELF FIRST

How come no one ever told me that I should be the first to get paid? For all those years I religiously paid my creditors first and routinely found myself with more month left at the end of the money and nothing left over to put into savings. Then I discovered a book called, "How to Wake up the Financial Genius inYou." In it, I was introduced to the idea of *paying myself first*.

Now, I'm not a financial consultant but I can assure you that the principle works. If you pay yourself *first* (put money aside for savings) and your creditors *second*, you'll build your savings and still find ways to pay your bills.

Why this works, I'm not exactly sure. All I can tell you is that seven years ago I never paid a bill until I received a pink notice(you know, the ones that say pay up today or loose a limb). I had checks bouncing everywhere. Several times a month, I was on the phone telling somebody to, *"Put it through again, it should clear this time."* Almost all of my creditors had hit men looking for me. Then I started paying myself *first* and my creditors *second*, and today, my savings account *and* my credit rating are very impressive.

They say that **"Some things must be believed to be seen"** —this is one of them.

13

TO GET MONEY
YOU CAN'T NEED IT

I've always thought that bankers were a hard breed to understand. Early on, I began to think of them as people who have committed the best years of their lives to developing the fine art of saying "no". You tell them all about yourself and why you need the money; they tell you why you can't have it.

The most important thing you need to know about bankers is that they need you. They have to and want to make loans, but they want to make safe loans. This is why they won't lend you money if they think you desperately need it. You see, they are afraid you won't be able to pay it back. So if you want to borrow money, you have to show them that you don't have to have it.

The trick is to borrow money when you really don't need it. That's right—borrow money when you have a a little extra cash. Go down to the bank and use the money you have as collateral on a loan, then pay it back as scheduled. By developing a relationship with your banker when you don't need money, you'll be able to get money from him when you do.

Trust me on this one—it works. Try it and soon your bankers will be giving you money, and *you won't even have to ask!*

14

THE 3 THINGS YOU NEED TO KNOW ABOUT MONEY

So I'm talking to an Anglo friend of mine the other day, who mentioned in passing that his five year old son made $22,000 last year doing commercials. What does a five year old do with twenty two thousand dollars, you ask? Why, he puts a couple thousand in savings and the remainder in certificates of deposits and stocks, of course. I quickly toyed with some figures and computed (without the benefit of a calculator) that if all things remain constant by age 7, this kid was going to be able to qualify for an American Express Gold Card. It further boggled my mind to realize that he would be starting his adult life with a working knowledge of things I hadn't fully understood till I was into my early thirties. Where did you learn about money?

A. The business section of the New York Times.

B. Your financial planner.

C. A class on money management.

D. Mom, dad, and Uncle Albert.

E. Personal experience.

If you're anything like me, a lot of what you learned about money came from relatives and personal experience.

And if your relatives are anything like mine, the entire scope of your education in money management was summed up in three lessons:

Lesson 1: The love of money is the root of all evil.

Lesson 2: 10% of all you earn should be given to the church in tithes.

Lesson 3: It will be easier for a camel to pass through the eye of a needle than for a rich man to get into the kingdom of heaven.

The central theme of the training was simple:

Don't waste time trying to make money and get wealthy, your reward will be in heaven (or something like that.) Now you understand why I spent the majority of my early adult life broke. I was just following God's will ...... or was I?

Though few church-going black folk I've met speak much about it, there were many rich men in the Bible—God-serving and deeply religious men like Abraham, Moses, and how about that guy Job? How did he get to be so wealthy, anyway? Stocks? Bonds? Mutual Funds? Why didn't we hear more about these guys?

The fact is that there's a lot about making money we weren't taught. So there's a lot of ignorance in the black community about money.

Take for example the idea that it takes money to make money. I can't count the number of times I've heard this misconception used as a reason why black people can't start their own businesses. The truth is that it doesn't take money to make money. It takes ideas.

In 1983, I was virtually penniless but that year I started a company with an idea—an idea that I sold to three investors. Each invested $600.00 a piece to create a company, a company that is today a multi-million dollar enterprise. This company continues to grow, but even now, its fuel is creativity not money.

There are billions of dollars out there looking for the next great idea to get behind. Since we're all capable of creating ideas, we all have the ability to raise and make money. But there are three things you'll have to do to successfully play the money game:

1. Accept that though the love of money is the root of all evil, a little money in the bank is desirable even unto the eyes of the Lord.

2. Realize that the Bible said it would be difficult for a rich man to enter the kingdom of heaven, but it didn't say it would be *impossible*!

3. Finally, if you're one of those people who still thinks it takes money to make money (and even if you aren't) go down to your local newsstand, grab a copy of every financial periodical you can get your hands on and start reading. When you're done, if you still believe it takes money to make money, come back and read the next chapter.

15

THIS IS YOUR MOST
VALUABLE POSSESSION

A very wise man observed that nothing is so powerful as clear ideas in the minds of enthusiastic and energetic men.

Your ideas are your most valuable possessions; they have the ability to bring into your life almost anything you desire.

Americans are fascinated with new ideas; they love new and creative approaches to old problems. Americans are always looking for a better mouse trap and are willing to reward creativity well. Ask Steven Jobs, Steven Spielberg, or Michael Jackson. Yes, one idea can make you rich. In fact, there are those of you who are flat broke today, but who ten years from now will be millionaires from one single idea.

Have you ever had an idea, on which you did a lot of thinking but not a lot of acting, only to wake up one morning and find that someone else had taken your idea and struck it rich? I've had it happen to me several times. (Most people don't know this but CNN's all news, 24 hours a day was my idea—no really!)

Each time I see someone else getting rich on one of *my* ideas, it reminds me that,

Ideas = money......*but only if we act on them.*

We're all capable of creating ideas! Lots of ideas! Millions of ideas! To turn a million ideas into a million dollars, we have to act on them. To start, you'll want to talk to people about them, and if that doesn't work, talk to more people. You see, to turn your ideas into money, you must begin by following the first commandment: DO SOME-THING, TRY SOMETHING, ANYTHING. And if what you try doesn't work, *try something else.*

16

YOU CAN TAKE THIS
TO THE BANK

I know you've heard it:

THE RICH GET RICHER WHILE
THE POOR GET POORER.

If you believe this, then you'll want to keep
reading.

I don't know why we place so little value on information. I just know that we do. The number
of black men who drop out of school, the few
who go on to college, and the priority we place
on entertainment over education all speak loudly
of how little we value information. But how
valuable is information really?

Well to some people on Wall Street, information
is so valuable they are willing to risk going to
jail for it, and they do. "But, those are white collar
criminals," you say. "Give me a better example."
Okay! How about the millions of people who
spend thousands of dollars each year (of their
hard earned money) on books, tapes, and seminars. What's wrong with these people? If school
is out, why do so many of them keep hitting the
books?

The answer is simple: they've discovered this very valuable and powerful secret:

THE INFORMED GET RICHER WHILE THE IGNORANT GET POORER

This great principle for accumulating wealth is used every day by the rich, yet it remains virtually unknown to many of us in the black community. So here it is, the secret revealed:

Value information like you value money and you'll have money!

17

THIS IS A FREE COUNTRY BUT NEVER UNDERESTIMATE THE POWER OF CASH

You have the right to live anywhere you want because this is a free country. Right? Well try to find a place to live in a nice neighborhood, and you'll quickly discover that though this is a free country, it takes money to buy that freedom.

You can find yourself without the most basic of freedoms unless you develop your purchasing power. By purchasing power, I mean your ability to buy freedom. You see, the freedom to live where you want, go where you want, and do what you want is more easily bought than legislated. It comes more quickly through dollars than it does through votes.

Some of us are confused. There are those who think "free country" means they don't have to work for anything; they think living the good life is constitutionally guaranteed.

However, what's really free in this county is free enterprise, and the more enterprising you are, the freer you're likely to be.

Sure, certain freedoms are guaranteed by the Constitution and the Bill of Rights, but let's consider freedom of speech for a moment. Yes, in America you can speak out about anything you want, but if you're trapped deep deep in an urban ghetto, no matter how loudly you speak, no one will hear you.

You see, it's money that talks in America. That's why those in power listen to the Arabs, the Japanese, and the Jews, and ignore where possible, the Blacks, the Hispanics, and the Indians. This also explains, why on Wall Street, when the Japanese spoke, E.F. Hutton listened.

Yes, freedom through politics is good, but as one company so eloquently put in a full page ad:

NEVER UNDERESTIMATE THE POWER OF CASH

Remember: Freedom is more easily bought than legislated.

18
ONLY IN AMERICA

"Only in America." That's what Don King says. Only in America are rags to riches stories a dime a dozen. Only in America could Reginald Lewis, the first black man to make a major impact on Wall Street, get into the arena with the big boys and walk away with close to 100 million dollars.

Only in America could a black boy like John Johnson grow up in complete poverty, borrow 500 dollars, start a publishing company, and end up with a net worth of over 150 million dollars.

Only in America could a man with a name like Wally Amos take something as commonplace as chocolate chip cookies, start a business, call it Famous Amos, and become incredibly wealthy.

What do all these black men have in common? They learned, played, and mastered the game of free enterprise. These men prove that the black man can go virtually anywhere he wants if he chooses the right game and learns how to play it—and the right game is free enterprise. Yes, this is the game you want to master.

The game of free enterprise is your vehicle to

freedom. It provides the playing field for those who are ready to rely on themselves to get what they want in life but to be a player, you must take it upon yourself to learn the game.

You'll want to find out how people start businesses with very little money; you'll want to know how they buy large assets with other people's capital; you'll want to learn all you can about how money is raised, made, and parlayed.

To do this you want to read and take classes.
Read and go to seminars.
Read and talk to business owners.

READ & READ & READ....

Don King is right, "Only in America," *but only if you learn the game.*

19

IF YOU THINK YOU FEEL THE SPIRIT, GET A SECOND OPINION

I was raised in the church, so I know what it means to walk by faith and not by sight. But I don't recall reading anywhere in the Bible that *"Thou shall succeed in business if thou will walk around blind without a cane."*

Over the years, I've met a number of deeply religious people who had scraped together what they could and went into business. Many had no business plans, no business experience, and no understanding of the industry they were entering. According to them, they were "stepping out on faith." Many of them invested their savings and mortgaged their homes. Some of them lost both.

Now, I know that the Lord works in mysterious ways, but I also know that it takes a lot of "know how" to succeed in business. So, if you think you hear "a voice from above" telling you to go into business (before you mortgage the farm) *get more information!*

20

GET ALL YOU CAN

"No way! If you think I'm gonna flip hamburgers at McDonalds for $4.50 an hour, you must be crazy," the brother said. His partner chimed in, "Word." A lot of black men think it's beneath them to take a job like that. I say "*think again.*"

I've held over 30 jobs in my life and was fired from all but one. I've cleaned toilets, loaded trucks, pleated skirts, delivered packages, waited on tables, collected money, sold hot dogs, and repaired computers—just to name a few. I hated every job I held, but from every job, I learned a valuable skill, and some valuable lessons about business, people and life.

I learned attention to detail from cleaning latrines in the Air Force—"clean enough to eat off of the floor"— that's what they wanted (and since you never knew if they might make you do it, you did your best to make them sparkle).

I learned job planning from loading trucks, customer service by waiting on tables, and effective phone skills from my job as a collector.

Each of these jobs paid meagerly and seemed *beneath* me at the time, but each contributed a valuable skill to my repertoire.

It was the combined skills collected from *all* of my work experiences that helped me to build a successful business of my own.

So if they want you to start as a janitor in the mailroom—do it! When you open your own business, that's one less thing you'll have to pay someone to teach you.

21
THE SUN WILL COME UP TOMORROW

If your mother is anything like mine, she has a way of saying things that stick to you like fly paper for the rest of your life. Things like: "So Errol, do you believe that you are right and the **whole** world is wrong," or things like, "one of these days you're going to wish you had listened to me." (How did she know that?) One of her favorite sayings was "stop eating like there is no tomorrow." It took a while for me to really understand what she meant by that, but once I did, I realized that her message is one that needs to be passed on.

Breaking the habit of eating, thinking, and living like there's no tomorrow is one of the biggest hurdles black men have to leap. You see, many of us tend to live for today. We're generally not inclined to invest in tomorrow. Perhaps it's because for many black men tomorrow hasn't offered much hope, but there can be no hope unless we learn to invest in the future.

When the president of a major Japanese firm was asked how far his company plans into the future, he replied, "250 years." Surprised, the interviewer asked "What does it take to carry out such long range goals?" He swiftly replied, "patience." This story demonstrates the Japanese inclination to plan for tomorrow and think in the long run— a quality we need to pick up and pick up fast.

I was 23, when I received my first solicitation to buy life insurance. To this day I still remember my initial response: *"Life Insurance? For what? So my wife and some other man can live high on the hog at my expense? Forget it."* It was 10 years before I would clearly see how short-sighted I had been. Ironically, I've grown to be exceptionally forward looking, constantly preparing for tomorrow and investing in a better future for myself and my family.

Investing in the future means going to work *today* to build something that can be "passed on". "Something like what?" you ask. Well my favorite choice is a family business. You see, for years families have started small businesses that have grown and been passed on, leaving each succeeding generation better off than the previous one. Whether it's a business, real estate, or a simple life insurance policy, building and passing on the wealth is a value that runs deep among the cultures that progress—a value that has turned families into dynasties.

You can be sure the sun will come up tomorrow, but the only way to be sure tomorrow will be any brighter than today, is to start *building something*....anything, that can be "passed on."

22

YOU CAN BE A BIG FISH IN A SMALL POND BUT ONLY THE RIVER FLOWS TO THE SEA

No matter how successful you are in the black community, you're missing out on enormous opportunities, unless you can operate in the mainstream.

America's most successful black men have the ability to cross over. They can operate effectively in both Black and White America.

Some of us see *cross over* as *compromise.* Many believe that those who do have "sold out," but learning to swim in the mainstream is a matter of simple arithmetic.

To stay out of the mainstream is to close the door on over 200 million opportunities to sell your products and services (and that's just in this country).

A key to the extraordinary rise of Japan as an economic power was their ability to sell their goods to millions of Americans. They would never have come so far so fast had they confined themselves to doing business just among their own people.

There is a huge sea of opportunity out there. To get to it, you have to jump into the mainstream. If not, at best *you'll be a big fish in a small pond*!

PART III

WHAT HOLDS BLACK MEN DOWN AND WHAT TO DO ABOUT IT

23
RESPECT

Question: What do black men have in common with Rodney Dangerfield?

Answer: The feeling that we get "no respect."

"Just a little bit," said Aretha Franklin. "R-E-S-P-E-C-T.... give it to me." To say that black men "have a thing" about respect is a monumental understatement. I hear black men on the street talking about it all the time. They talk about "dissin"people* , being "dissed", and "who dissed who". One prominent psychologist discovered that some black men are so concerned with respect, they're literally killing each other to get it.

Well, thanks to Aretha, we know how to spell it, but the grand prize question is how do we get it. The answer? You get respect the old fashioned way—you have to "earn" it. I know this might disappoint some of you, but the fact that we're *black and proud and said it loud* is not enough. The level of respect we get is connected to the level of respect we give. In other words, you get respect by giving respect.

*disrespected

When you give respect to:
>   yourself
>   your mate
>   your family
>   your possessions
>   your neighborhood
>   your neighbors
>   your work
>   your time
>   your abilities
>   your life
>   your contribution
>   your reputation
>   and your word,

you send a strong message out into the world
that says I give respect and I deserve it in return.

The more respect you give , the more you'll find
it rare that others will try to (as they say on the
street) *dis you!*

24
ONLY PLAY GAMES YOU CAN WIN

I was fascinated by a story I read the other day about Donald Trump and his crumbling empire. The article was taking Trump's moment of crisis to point out that in spite of his incredible success, in spite of all the trophies he had acquired, though he was once estimated to have a net worth of well over a billion dollars and considered to be one of the most powerful men in New York, Donald Trump never achieved the status and recognition he so desperately desired.

It seems that the members of a certain elite social club decided that Trump's dollars weren't good enough (even though he apparently had over one billion of them). Though Donald desperately wanted to be accepted into their very exclusive club, despite all of his efforts to achieve more status and prove his worthiness, he was never invited into their inner circle.

What Mr. Trump apparently did not understand is that desire for status is a *no-win game*. It's a game with a moving target. The closer you get to it, the farther away it moves. Moreover, people who have status maintain it by limiting the number of people with whom they share it. This is important to know because as black people we have a special craving for status. A craving based on a desire to attain some level of dignity and respect.

Well, let me *try* to save you some time and money. You see, I've spent a lot of money on status symbols, but they ultimately never brought me the prestige and status I thought they would. There was always somebody with a newer car, a nicer Rolex, or a bigger home.

Eventually, it became clear that the status game was a game I couldn't win. This was confirmed when I read about "the Donald" and realized that if Trump's billions couldn't buy it, I might as well keep my Trump, I mean chump change in my pocket.

I later discovered that I could best achieve the status I was striving to get by accepting and respecting myself—by recognizing my inherent dignity and self worth. *Now there's a game you can win!*

25

DON'T BUY IT
DON'T SELL IT

So what is racism anyway? Over the years I've heard a couple of definitions that I really liked. One man called it "a pigment of the imagination" while another, Ashley Montagu, called it "a confused and dangerous idea that one day would be seen for what it is."

Now I agree that racism is a confused idea, but I wonder if some of us will ever see it for what it is.

The truth is that racism is an illusion—an erroneous perception of reality. That's right... it's not real. So if you believe it is, then you have been fooled, but don't panic, you're not alone.

There are many people who have bought and sold the illusion of race—so many that the illusion has apparently become real. Every day millions of people make major decisions in their lives based on race. They decide whom to hire, where to shop, and where to live, based heavily on racial considerations.

A couple of years ago, I spoke with the manager of a large black entertainment firm here in Los

Angeles. He told me that it was his personal policy to only hire blacks. He called his policy affirmative action .... I called it racism.

You see, somewhere I heard that two wrongs don't make a right. So I don't believe in hiring a man because he's black. I hire a man because he's good.

Nor will I buy from a business because it's black owned. I buy from a business because they deliver quality products and services.

Likewise, I do not support programs because they are black programs, I support them because they are good programs.

The point there is simple: racism is a dangerous illusion. Afrocentricity is racism—don't buy it, don't sell it.

26

PUT THE BLACK MAN IN HIS PLACE

I think now is as good a time as any for us to straighten out our priorities. I've met men who were black men first and *husbands second*. I've met those who were black men first and *fathers second*. I've met men who were black men first and *professionals second*. Now this may not sit well with some of you but being a black man is not the most important thing you are. The fact that we are men of color is insignificant when compared to the other things that we are and must be.

It's time to transcend color and put the black man in his place.

Each of us is part of a larger race that demands our attention—it's called the human race. Every year we see more and more black men rise to positions of leadership and influence in part because they have learned to put their "blackness" in perspective.

Doug Wilder became the nation's first black governor not by running as a "black candidate" but by running as the "best candidate." David Dinkins did not become the first black mayor of

New York City by seeing himself as a "black leader" representing "black people" on "black issues," he presented himself as an "able leader" representing "all people" on issues important to all.

Sure, the fact that you are part of the black race is significant but your membership in the human race is more important. So when you go out into the world everyday, don't go as a black man ...

GO AS A MAN!

27

TO BE OR NOT TO BE
THE CHOICE IS YOURS

Everybody has some disadvantage in life. If you don't believe me, just stop a couple hundred people on the street and ask them. What you'll find is that almost everybody will claim that in some way, on some level, they carry a burden that others don't.

But this feeling has moved to a new level as group after group comes out of the closet to declare, "I too have been victimized."

There has never been a shortage of victims in the world but today, declaring oneself a victim is the latest fashion statement.

Homosexuals, alcoholics, overeaters, drug abusers, sexual abusers, those in the majority as well as those in the minority are all crying the "V" word.

Though all victims differ, they all agree on the ground rules. Here are the requirements you must meet to be a *card carrying victim* in good standing:

1. Declare yourself a victim.
2. See yourself as exploited, alienated, and powerless.
3. Make somebody or something else responsible for your condition. (Blame others.)
4. Wear the victim label on your forehead.
5. Carry the card with you at all times (you know, don't leave home without it).

Of course, membership has its privileges; they include sympathy and charity. But let's just say you're not interested in charity. Let's suppose you're one of those men who would rather be victorious than victimized, a cause rather than an effect! I'm speaking now to those of you who would rather win than whine. If you're among this group, then for you the rules are different. You must:

1. Declare yourself a *non*-victim.
2. See yourself as capable of controlling your circumstances.
3. Take full responsibility for changing your conditions.
4. Refuse to wear any and all victim labels.
5. Do what must be done to make your life better.

Ah! I think I've just found a simpler way to say this:

IF YOU DON'T THINK AND ACT LIKE A VICTIM, YOU WON'T BE ONE!

28

ALL OF THOSE BLACK MEN CAN'T BE WRONG

If you meet a black man who talks funny and seems to know very little about smothered chicken and collard greens, don't worry, he's not an Uncle Tom. He's probably one of the thousands of West Indian men who come to this country every year.

Like other immigrants, many of them have heard that America is the land of opportunity—a place where the streets are paved with gold. And just like the other immigrants who came here before them, *they* have come to get their share.

Once they arrive, they immediately go to work to build a secure life for themselves. Most are not briefed by the N.A.A.C.P. or the National Urban League about the many barriers that exist for black men in this country, *so they behave as if the barriers don't exist*. Many secure good jobs, invest in real estate, and open their own businesses. The barriers through which they break in the process are broken, because they are unaware of the limits, so they are not bound by them.

Denroy is one of those young black men. He's from the Carribbean and in 10 short years has managed to do quite well for himself. He owns a real estate brokerage, an escrow service, a mortgage company, a limousine service, and an office complex here in Los Angeles. (Not bad for a guy who's dark enough to be discriminated against by everybody including his own people.)

Talk to Denroy about the barriers that hold black men back, and he's unusually quiet; you see, Denroy doesn't believe in barriers. He's among a group of black men who believe and have proven that many of us set our own barriers— that most black men are *holding themselves back.*

"Ah come on; give me a break" you say. I've been trying to get ahead in this country all my life. I've seen what the white man is doing, so don't tell me what's holding me back—I know!" Well maybe you do and maybe you don't (by the way, this is a good time to take a deep breath and count to ten).

I recall a story I was told a couple of years ago about how elephants are trained. I'm told that when they are very young they are attached to a chain that is connected to a stake, which is driven deep into the ground. At first, they pull, tug and struggle to break free of the chain, till finally they conclude they can't break free —and give up.

The baby elephant grows to be a massive and powerful beast. But the trainers continue to contain it with a tiny chain attached to a stake. At any time, the elephant could set himself free, but he continues to operate within his limits, because he has long since been convinced that he is being held back and can't break free!

Could it be that black men are really holding themselves back? I'll let you answer that one for yourself. All I can say is, *all of those successful West Indians can't be wrong!*

29
REAL MEN ARE...

Do you know what makes a real man?
Let me tell you what it's not:

- It's not how fine his wardrobe, how hip his haircut, or how nice his car.
- It's not how far or fast he can run, how much weight he can lift, or how many baskets he can sink in your face.
- It's not how many status symbols he possesses, how many women he sleeps with or how many names he can pluck from his little black book.
- It's not how large his muscles are, his sexual organ, or his bank account.
- It's not how big his title, his ego, or his position in life.
- It's not how many initiation tests he passes, to what groups he belongs, or what rank he achieves.
- It's not how many businesses he owns, how many people he controls, or how many adversaries and competitors he has conquered.

THE TRUE TEST OF A MAN IS HOW COM-
FORTABLE AND SECURE HE IS WITHIN
HIMSELF

Black America Needs Real Men!

30
WHAT YOU EXPECT
IS WHAT YOU GET

The story is told of two black men relocating from Los Angeles to San Jose. On the way in, both stopped at the local gas station on the outskirts of town. As the attendant serviced the first man's car, the man mentioned that he was new to the city and asked what he could expect from the people there. The attendant responded with a question, "What were the people like in the city you just left?" "Oh they hated blacks," said the man, "they were cold, bigoted, and extremely racist." The attendant then informed the man that "The people in San Jose are very much like that," as he collected for the gas and watched the man go on his way.

Shortly thereafter came the second man who asked the very same question. Just as he did with the first man, the attendant responded with a question, "What were the people like in the city you just left?" "Very friendly" said the second man, "warm and extremely helpful." As the attendant took the second man's money, he informed him, "The people in San Jose are very much like that."

It's become very clear to me that to a great degree, we get what we expect. I've gone as far as to intentionally manipulate my expectations just to test the credibility of this principle.

I quickly found that the way people responded to me was sometimes totally controlled by how I expected them to respond.

I further discovered that depending on my expectations, I could change good situations into bad and bad situations in to very good ones.

Once you have experienced this yourself, you'll understand why it's so important to manage your expectations.

The key is "positive expectancy," By this, I mean you must make it a habit to expect the best.

Expect to be respected.
Expect to be treated with dignity.
Expect to be accepted.
Expect to be treated fairly.

Will this work all the time? Of course not. But you'll significantly improve how well you are treated, the more you expect to be treated well.

31

20 REASONS TO BELIEVE IN THE IMPOSSIBLE

There are many reasons to believe that you can't make it in this country and if you happen to be one of those black men who collects them, you know exactly what I mean. There is discrimination in the educational system, in the political system, and the job market. There is racism in the government, in the police department, and in the media. All of which can make it pretty easy to believe that it's "impossible" for a black man to succeed in this country. But today I'd like to give you 20 reasons to *believe in the impossible*:

Tom Bradley	Spike Lee
Wally Amos	Muhammad Ali
Reginald Lewis	Robert Townsend
David Dinkins	Berry Gordy
Alex Haley	Ed Bradley
Colin Powell	William Gray
Bryant Gumbel	Arsenio Hall
Bernard Shaw	Jesse Jackson
Ron Brown	Ron Johnson
Andrew Young	Willie Brown

All of these black men have achieved and accomplished things that many of us would have sworn were *impossible.* Yet, these men all play on the same field as we do, and despite how unlevel it might be, they have succeeded.

A veteran member of the NAACP stood up one afternoon during on of my seminars and declared that one of the reasons black people can't get ahead is because "whites won't buy from black businesses." He strongly believed he was right. I strongly disagreed with him. And evidently so did the thousands of "whites" who have bought my products and services over the years!

YOU'VE GOT TO BELIEVE!

32

HE WHO DIES WITH THE MOST GOLD CHAINS WINS

If life is a game, then what's the objective? How do you know when you've won? My thoughts on this have changed several times over the years.

When I was very young, "dance" was the name of the game. He who had the most moves won. Later sports became the arena, and it was he who had the most trophies who could claim victory. Then we discovered the opposite sex, and life became a contest to pursue and conquer more girls than any man within a 20 mile radius.

As I look out at the spectrum of black men today, it's clear that many of us are still struggling to figure out the game and define a way to keep score. The current games indicate that the stakes have gone up considerably. The options now include: he who sells the most drugs wins, he who shoots the most people wins, and currently enjoying strong popularity is he who dies with the most gold chains wins. (Of course, he who can pursue and conquer the most women is still a favorite choice).

I'd be remiss if I didn't acknowledge that many

of us have progressed beyond this point and are now playing in the major league where the name of the game is to get the best position, move into the best neighborhood, and make the most money.

Unfortunately, it will take years for many of us to discover that it's:

He who gets the most out of life
While giving something back that really wins!

33

GET OUT OF THE MINOR LEAGUE AND START "LIVING LARGE"

If you have to think anyway, you might as well think big. That's how Donald Trump put it, and in spite of his troubles, I'd say this is still pretty good advice.

Back on the block, our young men call it "Livin' Large", and though their interpretation clearly needs a little refinement, it's good to see they are thinking bigger than I did at their age.

During my six years in the Air Force, I had an opportunity to go to Japan, Germany, and England, but I did all I could to weasel out of these assignments. Why? Because my life revolved around the night life in New York City, and I didn't want to leave. I'll never know what opportunities I missed as a result of my limited vision and minor league thinking.

There are many of us who are limited by midget-mindedness. We think small and operate on a small scale. We've missed out on many opportunities around our cities, around the country, and around the world by keeping our attention focused on the immediate black community.

There is an incredible amount of life that exists beyond the black community. There are opportunities everywhere but to take advantage of them, we have to look beyond our families, our friends, our churches, and our neighborhoods to see what's shaping up in the world around us.

You see, the world is planning a big party. It's called the new world order and even the communists are invited. At the party, they'll be defining the key players in a new world community. Now, I understand why we missed the first party, but I'd hate to see us miss this one.

To attend, it's going to take some major league ambition, major league vision, and some major league action which all begins with major league thinking.

The kind of major league thinking it took for David Dinkins to aspire to be mayor or New York. The kind of thinking behind Reginald Lewis' purchase of Beatrice Foods. The type of major league thought that took Jesse Jackson to Iraq to free American hostages.

These men are major league thinkers whose actions created major league achievements. By their actions, they are showing all of us what it really means to "live large."

I don't care where you're starting, think big!

34
POWER AND INFLUENCE: YOU HAVE TO HAVE THE JUICE

Power is a subject I learn more and more about every day. Most of my early lessons were centered on how to get power and how to keep it. During that period, I discovered that there are four types of power.

Reward Power - the ability of an individual or group to withhold rewards (you know, the power most women have over us).

Coercive Power - the ability of an individual or group to punish, discipline, or adversely affect. The police have this power.

Referent Power - the power that comes from being close to a source of power. Agents to stars and executive secretaries fit into this category.

Expert Power - the power that comes when you can do something better than others. (We can assume that Michael Jordon commands a considerable amount of this power.)

Like Tom Bradley and Marion Barry, more and more black men are rising to positions of power.

As they do, they face a new challenge:

"Now that I have power, what am I going to do with it?"

Just in case you weren't sure, the idea that *power corrupts* applies to black men as well as whites. So when many of us find ourselves having power over people (often for the first time in our lives) we abuse it.

During my Air Force basic training, I was assigned the lofty position of dorm chief. This meant that when the drill sergeant was not around, I was in charge. In my squadron, there were at least 30 men, and at age 18, it was the first time I had ever been given so much power over so many people.

I had always enjoyed marching, but there was something about watching our drill sergeant call cadence that gave me a special thrill. So one afternoon, I decided to exercise the power of my new position. I called the squadron to attention and proceeded to march them across the base.

Ah! What a power trip! There I was in all my glory, calling cadence from the drill sergeant's position. Hut 2..3..4.. Hut ..2..3.. Suddenly a voice from out of the blue yelled, *"Squadron Halt!"* The voice and the firm hand on my shoulder was that of the assistant drill sergeant. *"What in the hell do you think you are doing airman."*

His voice was like thunder, and as I looked into his steely eyes, I suspected that my rapid rise to power would soon be coming to an end..I was right!!

Yes, we definitely need to know something about managing power. We need to know that though power is necessary, influence is more important. Influence comes from developing admirable qualities. When you can be trusted, when you show fairness and good judgment, when your word is good, and you demonstrate integrity. When you establish your ability to get things done, then you'll have the real juice— *influence.*

35

DON'T GET LOST
IN THE MASQUERADE

The meeting was set for Saturday morning at 8:00 a.m. sharp! About ten of us were meeting to take a group portrait for a promotional brochure. Most of us had never met. All of us were busy black professionals. Everyone showed up on time except one young man. Since they tell me I'm supposed to change the names to protect the innocent, let's just call this young man, Brad. As we waited for Brad, we used the time to get acquainted but after 30 very social minutes, he still had not arrived.

A few of us were just beginning to get anxious, when a late model luxury car pulled into the parking lot. Yes, it was Brad. We watched him slowly drive up to where we all were standing. He then backed into a parking space, where he (very conspicuously) spent another five minutes on his car phone. Patiently we all stood by watching. We would end up spending about an hour together that morning, a good part of which Brad had his portable phone to his ear. However, he didn't do much talking which led me to believe that his *silent partner* must have suddenly had a lot to say.

It was clear to most that Brad was doing all he could to look important, but from my viewpoint, Brad had simply *lost himself* in the masquerade.

One man said "the more prosperous we become, the more preposterous we become." I've witnessed enough of this to agree with him.

Some of us mysteriously develop exotic accents, while others forget how to use monosyllabic words. I've been to black functions where the pretentiousness was so thick it was hard to breathe.

But I've found that the most successful people I've ever met were secure enough to be whoever they really are. So whatever you do on your way to the top, please don't get lost in the masquerade.

BE YOURSELF!

36

THE SHORTCUT
TO DISTINCTION

Question: What do Willie Brown,
         Oprah Winfrey, and
         Bryant Gumbel have
         in common?

. Answer: The ability to speak well.

"The ability to speak effectively is the short cut
to distinction." That's what Dale Carnegie said.
And though I didn't fully understand what he
meant at the time, I was always interested in
short cuts, so I decided to read his book. As I
read, I became fascinated with the things Mr.
Carnegie claimed the ability to communicate
could achieve. So fascinated, that I would ultimately make it a lifelong study.

Look around you. Those who can communicate
succeed. The ability to get in touch with others,
and to effectively put into words ideas, and
feelings which people from various backgrounds
can understand, is a quality many successful
black men share.

I got my first glimpse of this from watching the
pastor of my church. What an incredible ability

he had to reach out and talk to people. This quality *clearly* seemed to distinguish him wherever he went. I remember watching him step in to handle a problem one of our church members was having at the famous Waldorf Astoria Hotel in New York. Though I never quite figured out what all the commotion was about, I did notice that as soon as he began to speak, the man behind the desk settled down and became very cooperative. I immediately thought to myself, "I want to be able to do that."

But it would be years later before I would find out what "that" was. It was the ability to talk to people and handle people at all levels.

Whatever you're planning to do with your life, the better you communicate, the more success-ful you'll be. So learn to speak well—it's still the shortest path to distinction.

37

IF THERE IS A "NATE"
IN YOUR LIFE
DON'T LISTEN TO HIM

"Whatever you do, never trust a white man."
That was the warning I received from my best
friend, Nate some 20 years ago.

He was just passing on these words of caution,
as they had been handed down to him from his
father.

Every so often, I reflect back to his warning and
consider how glad I am that I didn't listen to him.
You see, some of the best relationships I've had
in my life have been with whites (but it doesn't
stop there). Many of the *best experiences* I've had
on many levels have been with people from
various other cultures.

The best secretary I've ever had was Filipino. The
most reliable contractor I've had was Mexican.
The most dependable employee I've ever had
was Armenian, the best sales person I've ever
had was Columbian, the best telemarketing
representative I've ever had was from India.

Over the years, experiences like these have made

me a strong believer in tapping the best in all cultures.

Now I know there are those who will read this and immediately send up a prayer for the "poor brother who has lost touch with the needs of his people," but I'm praying too, that one day my people will accept that anyone who preaches hate and distrust (no matter how it's disguised or justified) does not serve our best interest. I'm praying that one day we'll recognize that what's *good for the human race*, is what's *good for our race*.

Yes, everyday I'm praying, that hopefully in my lifetime, *people will trust people* based on the content of their character and not by the color of their skin.

PART IV

A FEW MORE THINGS...

SOME QUICKIES

QUICKIE 1

FORGET THE EXPERIENCE BUT GRAB THE LESSONS

For many of us, the thought of making a mistake, being wrong, or failing at something we try, can be paralyzing. Often, we're so afraid of striking out that we hesitate to even pick up the bat and swing. But to succeed, you must be willing to strike out—that's right. You have to make it okay to fail. This is vital, because if you make it okay to fail, it becomes okay to *try* and it's the number of *tries* that count.

You see, one of the common qualities among those who succeed is a willingness to experiment—to put themselves and their ideas to the test to see if they work. If it doesn't work they say, "Okay, that was a good lesson. I'll never do it *that way* again." But instead, many of us say, "I'll never *do it* again". I'll never get married again." I'll never take anybody's advice again." I'll never try to start another business again."

These people tend to overlook the valuable lessons to be learned from their failures, but hold on to their awful experiences for life. But the key to success is to: *Forget your experiences, grab the lessons, and keep on swinging!*

QUICKIE 2

HE WHO HAS THE PLAN WINS!

Has anything like this ever happened to you? A group of your friends are getting together and you're all trying to decide where to go for dinner. You are not sure where you want to go or what you feel like eating, but someone else in the group knows *exactly where* they want to go, and *exactly what* they want to eat. Minutes later (and much to your surprise) you find yourself in some strange restaurant, sitting on the floor, eating Moroccan food with your hands, asking yourself, "How in the world did I ever get talked into this one." That's how life is—the man with the plan wins.

If you don't make a choice in life, someone else will choose for you. There are millions of people out there and many of them have plans for your life. Without a plan of your own, you run the risk of waking up one day, and finding out that you've ended up where somebody else wanted you to go!

QUICKIE 3

YOU NEED 20/20 VISION

Vision is the ability to see what others can't see. The ability to keep your eyes on the goal in spite of the circumstances around you.

The story is told of two prisoners in one small cell who had no light, except the little bit coming through a very tiny window. Though both men spent a lot of time gazing at the window, they each saw different things.

One of them saw the ugly iron bars, which constantly reminded him of his imprisonment. As he stared at these bars, day after day, he became bitter, discouraged, and hopeless. But the other prisoner looked *through* the bars and saw the stars beyond. As he gazed up at those stars, he found himself filled with hope, thinking of the day he would be released to start a new life. Though the prisoners were looking at the same window, *one saw bars while the other saw stars*. The difference in their vision made the difference in their lives.

When the going gets tough, hold your vision!

QUICKIE 4

THINK LIKE A MASTER
WORK LIKE A SLAVE

The people I've met who were masters in their field were people who were willing to D.W.I.T. (Do Whatever It Takes) to accomplish their goals. They were willing to pay their dues and work like slaves if necessary. Many were willing to do this because they believed in a simple principle:

If you work like few people will for five years, you can live like few people can for the rest of your life!

QUICKIE 5

THE SWEET SMELL OF SUCCESS DOESN'T HAPPEN OVERNIGHT.

If you're like most people, you want everything now! I understand that because I'm very impatient myself. I'm like the guy who prayed "Dear Lord, please give me patience, and I want it now!"

Wouldn't it be great if life were like a T.V. mini-series.

You're born at 8:00 p.m. (Prime Time). By 8:15 p.m. you're adopted by rich parents and become sole heir to the family millions. By 8:30 p.m., you're the wealthiest, healthiest person in the neighborhood, and members of the opposite sex are throwing themselves at you at a rate of 3 per minute. It's time for a commercial now but we'll be back in two minutes and two seconds. After the station break, you parlay the family millions into billions in a hostile take over, leaving just enough time for you to meet the woman of your dreams, and ride off into the sunset before the eleven o'clock news.

It would be great if life were that way, *but it ain't!*

QUICKIE 6

HANG TOUGH

Looking back on your life, what do you wish you had not quit.

- Do you wish you had finished college or graduate school?
- Do you wish you had maintained that relationship?
- Do you wish you had held on to that investment when the going got tough?

Whatever the game, you'll find that *when the going gets tough, most people leave.* For this reason, I believe that bad times are the best times to make it because that's when those who aren't mentally prepared to go the distance, drop out of the race.

When the race gets tough, and I feel like quitting, I watch a video tape of Dr. King. Every time I see him standing at the podium, after all he had faced (angry dogs, fire hoses, imprisonment, violent mobs) and hear him say, "We've come too far now—we ain't gonna let nobody turn us around," I am instantly inspired to persist in my life . I'm inspired to press on, to not let life's little problems turn me around. I'm encouraged to hang tough, to hang in there, and in the words of Winston Churchill, to *"Never, Never, Never Give Up."*

QUICKIE 7

PERFORMANCE IS EVERYTHING

Most people have a hard time getting themselves to take action though they really have good intentions. They really intend to *go on that diet*, they *really plan to start a business*, but for some reason, they just can't seem to get themselves to move on it today. It's as if they have one foot on the gas and the other on the brake—the mind says go but the body says no. They're stuck!

If you are going to live the life you desire, you'll have to get yourself to act because *successful living demands action*, consistent action, bold and immediate action!

This means you don't have a lot of time to talk about what you are *going to do*. You have to get busy doing it. It means you must feel a sense of urgency in your life. So while some people live like they have another 50 years, you'll want to live like you have just another 50 minutes.

The world is overrun with talented people who intend to do *big things* tomorrow. But you must commit to do big things *today*!

You see, some people judge themselves by what they feel they are capable of doing but the world judges us by what we have done—*performance is everything!*

QUICKIE 8

"IT" CAN DO A LOT MORE THAN SELL FOOTWEAR

"Just Do It." What a simple and powerful message. But I can't tell you what "it" means. Because only *you* know what "it" is.

What I *can* tell you is that it's the thing you've been thinking about doing—the thing you really need to do. It's the thing you know you should be doing that you've put off doing for years. (Do you see "it" now? ....Yes, that thing.)

If you really want to make it, you should go home tonight and do this: make a list of the five things you least want to do that would change your life if you did them. Pick the first one and *start doing it*.

QUICKIE 9

IF IT SOUNDS TOO GOOD TO BE TRUE...

I was the ultimate sucker for a get rich quick scheme. So when I received a letter from a company who said they had evaluated my invention and thought it had "enormous profit potential," I was much too excited too even consider checking out the company. I drove over one thousand miles and spent five thousand dollars to learn a very valuable lesson. You see, I never realized any of those "enormous profits," (nor did I get my five thousand dollars back).

People spend millions of dollars every year trying to get rich quick. Las Vegas, Atlantic City, and the lottery are magnets for those who hope to go to bed poor and wake up rich.

Occasionally it happens but for the most part I've found that *if it sounds too good to be true, it probably is.*

V

ONE LAST THING. . .

LOOK INTO YOUR HANDS

Turn your palms to the sky and look into your hands. What do you see? (Please don't say dirty hands). Look a little longer. I hope you see your future because that's where it is—in your hands. Throughout these pages there is a consistent message. The message is that *the future of black men is in the hands of black men*. This is the secret that has eluded black men for years; it is by far the most important thing every black man needs to know.

Each of us has the ability to create our own opportunities, pull our own strings, and affect our own future. We are only locked out if we assume we are unable to open the door.

James Brown *almost* had it right when he sang, "I don't want nobody to give me nothing—open up the door I'll get it myself." If you listened to James, you were headed in the right direction, but you'll need one minor change to be on the right track.

OPEN YOUR OWN DOORS!

As you look for the key to open those doors, look into your own hands, and even if you don't immediately see it there, don't look anywhere else. You see it's definitely there—in your hands, so keep staring at your palms until you find it.